America Is Voting

Written by Judy Dashman

Table of Contents

Introduction

Americans vote on everything—from who plays in the All-Star baseball game to who becomes president of the United States. Voting gives people a chance to have an equal say in things that are important to them.

In this book, you will read about voting and how it affects your life.

Baseball fans voted for their favorite players to play on the 2005 American League All-Star team.

Republican National Convention 2004

3

The Story of Voting

Long ago, most of the world was ruled by kings and queens and tyrants—including the American colonies. They were ruled by George III, king of England, until they won their freedom in 1776.

The U.S. Constitution protects people's right to vote.

Americans fought the Revolutionary War for eight years before gaining their freedom.

Patrick Henry delivered a speech that helped rally the colonies to fight the Revolution.

.IBERTY, OR GIVE ME DEATH !"

Most Americans never wanted to be ruled by a king again, so they created a **democracy.** Now they could choose their leaders and have a say in how the country was run. At the heart of this new democracy was the right to vote.

At first, only a small group of wealthy men could vote in an **election.** Many people thought this was unfair. So they fought to change the law.

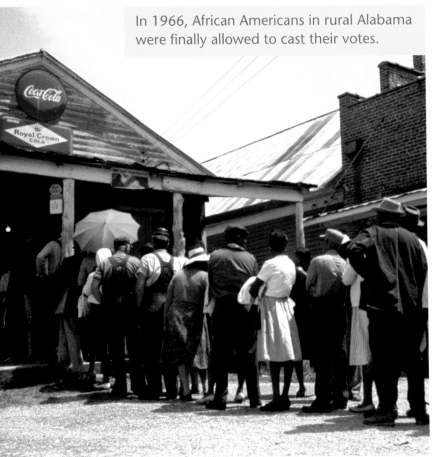

In 1966, African Americans in rural Alabama were finally allowed to cast their votes.

Voting Time Line	1776	1870
	Most white male landowners over 21 could vote.	African American men over 21 gained the vote.

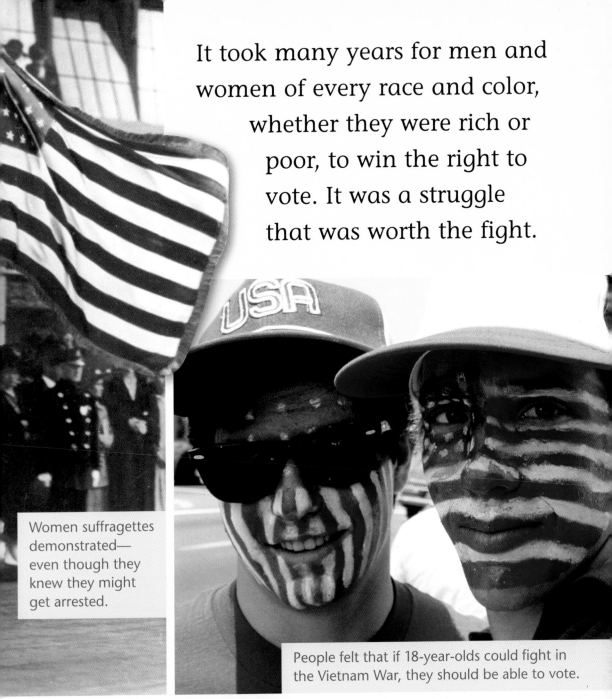

It took many years for men and women of every race and color, whether they were rich or poor, to win the right to vote. It was a struggle that was worth the fight.

Women suffragettes demonstrated—even though they knew they might get arrested.

People felt that if 18-year-olds could fight in the Vietnam War, they should be able to vote.

1920

Women over 21 gained the vote.

1962

Native Americans over 21 could vote in all 50 states.

1971

Voting age lowered to 18 years.

Every Vote Counts!★

Surprisingly, millions of people choose not to vote. They think their one vote won't make a difference. What do you think?

Many kids think that it is important to vote, and they're doing something about it. Some kids are joining the organization Kids Voting USA. They follow the elections and talk about the candidates with adult family members and friends. These kids have been very successful in getting "stay at home" voters to the **polls.** You can do that, too!

Many kids learn about voting by going to the polls.

A majority vote in a classroom can help a teacher decide which book to read aloud.

Lower Voter Turnout

In recent elections, many Americans who are able to vote rarely—or never—cast a ballot. Lack of interest in the issues and distrust in the candidates are two reasons that less than 65 percent of Americans voted in the 2004 presidential election.

There are many types of elections. Local elections take place in the town where you live. In a local election, you might vote to elect a new mayor or vote on whether or not to hire more firefighters.

In state and national elections, you vote for people who will represent you either in your state legislature or in our nation's capital, Washington, D.C. You might even vote for the president. The president is the only official voted on by all Americans.

Dianne Feinstein was the first woman from California to be elected to the U.S. Senate.

Sometimes people vote to buy new equipment for their town.

National Officials

Office	Term	Number
Representative	2 years	435
Senator	6 years	100
President	4 years	1
Supreme Court Justice (appointed)	Lifetime	9

Election Time

People vote for a **candidate** because they share similar ideas about issues. It takes months of campaigning for candidates to get their ideas to the people. They run ads on TV, give speeches at rallies, and debate candidates from other **parties.**

Candidates on a whistle-stop campaign make brief speeches along the way.

In 1960, John F. Kennedy and Richard Nixon took part in the first televised presidential debates.

After all this, it's Election Day and the candidates wait for the people to make their choice. People have followed the campaigns, listened to the speeches, and talked about the issues. Now it's time for voters to make up their minds.

For a national election, voting takes place on the same day all across the country. Polling places are opened at schools, churches, and town buildings. Some are open from early morning to late at night. When the polls close, that's it—the election is over. People wait for the votes to be counted. Some voting machines count the **ballots** automatically, but others are counted by hand.

Secret ballots let people vote in private so no one can influence their decision.

BALLOT BOX
608

Thousands of people witnessed the swearing in of President Bush at the presidential inauguration in 2005.

John Kerry
PRESIDENT
www.JohnKerry.com

A disappointed supporter

Many people stay awake all night waiting for the election results. There's a lot of celebrating when a candidate wins. Your side may not win every election, but in a democracy, you'll get to vote again.

Families, schools, and groups are working together to learn about the importance of voting. How would you spread the word to get others out to vote?